MULTIPLE SIDE HUSTLES

STEP BY STEP GUIDE TO ACHIEVING FINANCIAL FREEDOM

BY BRETT STANDARD

Legal & Disclaimer

The information contained in this book and its contents is not designed to replace or take the place of any form of medical or professional advice; and is not meant to replace the need for independent medical, financial, legal or other professional advice or services, as may be required. The content and information in this book have been provided for educational and entertainment purposes only.

The content and information contained in this book has been compiled from sources deemed reliable, and it is accurate to the best of the Author's knowledge, information and belief. However, the Author cannot guarantee its accuracy and validity and cannot be held liable for any errors and/or omissions. Further, changes are periodically made to this book as and when needed. Where appropriate and/or necessary, you must consult a professional (including but not limited to your doctor, attorney, financial advisor or such other professional advisor) before using any of the suggested remedies, techniques, or information in this book.

Upon using the contents and information contained in this book, you agree to hold harmless the Author from and against any damages, costs, and expenses, including any legal fees potentially resulting from the application of any of the information provided by this book. This disclaimer applies to any loss, damages or injury caused by the use and application, whether directly or indirectly, of any advice or information presented, whether for breach of contract, tort, negligence, personal injury, criminal intent, or under any other cause of action.

You agree to accept all risks of using the information presented inside this book.

You agree that by continuing to read this book, where appropriate and/or necessary, you shall consult a professional (including but not limited to your doctor, attorney, or financial advisor or such other advisor as needed) before using any of the suggested remedies, techniques, or information in this book.

Table of Contents

INTRODUCTION

Achieving financial freedom is difficult because it is difficult to understand. When you ask most people what financial freedom means, you will typically get responses like "being rich", or the ability to purchase items they cannot afford today.

This view has destined many Americans to a lifetime of debt servitude and living paycheck to paycheck. The true way to achieve financial freedom is wealth creation. Unfortunately, if the term 'financial freedom' is vague for people, then the term 'wealth creation' might as well be a wholly different language. The first step to creating wealth is teaching people what it is.

Passive income is a form of income that a person receives over time for a one-time effort. The insurance industry is a good example of this. An agent may spend a few hours with you and sell you a life insurance policy. He will receive a commission when that policy is issued and every year at renewal. Note that he may not even give you a phone call after that initial meeting has taken place. So, as long as you renew your policy, the agent gets paid several times for a one-time effort.

The idea behind passive income is that you put a decent amount of work in at the beginning of your project so that you do not have to worry about putting a lot of work (or any work, in some cases) into your business in the future.

You will be able to simply sit back and collect the money that you worked hard for in the future.

Passive income simply explained is putting in the majority of the work once and then having the steady cash flow for months, years and sometimes even decades with a just a little of maintenance work from time to time. This way of earning an income gives you more time to build more passive income streams and this will, in turn, make you more and more money over time. A day job, however, is purely trading your time for a certain amount of money without any opportunity of scaling up. There is a ton of different methods to earning a passive income.

The trick is to start as early as possible. Investing takes time and effort - it is not a get-rich-quick or get-rich-overnight scheme. You can learn a lot about investing smartly and successfully in this book, and make huge profits by undertaking any passive income strategy of your choice.

CHAPTER 1

MULTIPLE SIDE HUSTLES

The goal of multiple side hustles is to live a life where your side hustles pay for your daily expenses until you have enough savings to invest (1-2 years).

Every investor has a different income and thus some have more to invest in their funds. Thus, the amount that different people contribute to their investment fund can vary wildly. To take full advantage of compound interest and other factors, exactly how much should you be investing?

As with everything in investing, there is no correct answer for every individual. The common answer is 10% of your income, meaning every paycheck 10% of it should be set aside and used only for adding to your portfolio. Aim for this number in general, as it is an easy sum to remember in addition to adding a decent amount every month.

However, if you can afford to add more than 10%, it is highly recommended that you do so. Tax-deferred accounts such as 401K and IRAs have a limited amount that can be put in every year, and maxing out that amount is a fantastic problem to have. Therefore, investing above and beyond that limit (in other accounts) is risky because of potential taxes, but well worth it if you can ensure high gains. Refer to the section on taxes to understand how to allocate your funds.

Compound interest favors large amounts of money, so putting in extra every month will definitely increase the output of your funds. Every month add 10%, or everything you feel comfortable investing.

Airbnb

Airbnb is like our human population - it just keeps growing.

With 100 million users and 640,000 hosts worldwide, Airbnb has opened a whole new market for homeowners and travelers.

Every day, homeowners are making extra cash from their spare rooms while travelers get a bed for a night at an affordable price.

But with over 2.3 million listings in 191 countries worldwide, there's a lot of competition...

Therefore, it's important you optimize your Airbnb listing to maximize your discoverability.

After all, you can't persuade potential guests to book with you if they can't find you.

So how do you go about optimizing your Airbnb listing?

Well, besides having great photos, getting positive reviews, and being a super host, one of the best ways to optimize your listing is having a great description.

An effective description hooks your readers, draws them in, and compels them to book with you. However, a poor description creates a bad image and kills inquiries and bookings.

If you can infuse your Airbnb description with persuasive copy, you'll be maximizing the chances of interested guests finding and staying with you.

But most hosts fail to realize the importance of having a great description for their listing.

Your title, summary, and description are some of the few areas in your listing that you can optimize to improve your conversions and bookings. After all, if you can't convince potential guests to book with you, your Airbnb business is going to fail no matter how hard you try.

Your Airbnb listing has to entice visitors and convince them that your place is what they need for their vacation.

Think of your Airbnb listing as your personal salesperson for your place. Once you have it up there, it's selling your place 24 hours a day 7 days a week.

So, you want to make sure it's doing the best job by equipping it with an attention-grabbing title, persuasive summary, and an irresistible description.

Effectively positioning yourself in the marketplace has helped me stand out from the crowd.

Making yourself visible will attract more customers. Also, great positioning will help make an impression to your customers.

If you look at the top brands, you'll notice that they position themselves well in their market. Creating unique image of themselves to set them apart from others. With this result, they're able to attract more followers who are will to pay for their products or services.

For example, Airbnb has positioned itself as a viable hospitality option for travelers who want a more personalized travel experience. At the same time, the Airbnb platform has created a unique opportunity for hosts to earn some extra money by renting out a spare room.

Another example of effective positioning is the Ritz-Carlton Hotel. Their suites are well known for being some of the most expensive places to stay in the world. Their reputation allow them to price their rooms a lot higher than a normal hotel rooms which include 91 luxury hotels and resorts worldwide.

In fact, the Ritz-Carlton Suite in Tokyo is an eye-popping $26,300 a night which sits on top of the tallest skyscrapers in Tokyo. The luxurious suite includes an oversized marble bathroom, individual rain shower booth, and an amazing view of the Imperial Palace and Mount Fuji.

The high price point and exclusive features show customers they are paying for a premium experience. This is backed up by basic human psychology that equates a higher price with better quality.

The Ritz-Carlton has positioned itself to certain customers, most notably wealthier people, who are better off financially. If they tried to target other types of customers, such as those with less money, it would have to reduce its prices, which would undermine its premium brand image.

Effective Positioning & How to Develop Your Unique Selling Proposition

To maximize your chances of succeeding on Airbnb, you have to effectively position your place so that it stands out from similar ones in your area.

Effective positioning should clearly communicate:

- Your brand's and product's/service's unique characteristics. In your case, your brand would be YOU (the host) and your product or service would be your place.

- How your place is different from competitors. What makes it special?

- How your place addresses your target customer's needs and problems.

One effective way to position is using USP. Basically, this will give you an advantange to place an offer and it'll be clear and concise.

For example, you can position your place as the perfect romantic getaway for young couples or the ideal place to get work done for a businessman. There are tons of ways you can position yourself.

What's the best way to position yourself?

By conducting market research. Ask your guests why they chose to stay at your place, what they liked and disliked, and their experiences with it. If you have your own website, you can conduct surveys or email your past guests who have signed up for your newsletter.

If you're still fairly new and have limited customers. Do some research and check your competitor to see if you can find a better position so that prospect will be more interest in you.

Chances are there's going to be many other places in your area that are vying for guests to book with them. Positioning is very essential since you should position yourself in a place where your competitors are showing signs of weakness.

If your competition are competing against price, then you should try to look into it at a different angle. place as having better amenities. Or you can position your place as a safe and relaxing place for families with young children. Or you can highlight the fact that your place is located in the heart of downtown where guests can check out all the trendiest bars.

Finding a Roommate

Part 1 - The First Step: Critical Things to Do Before You Start Looking or Advertising for a Roommate

Before you start advertising or looking for a roommate, there are some things you should do in order to help you cut down on wasted time, energy, money and resource spent on the wrong people. The old saying from Shakespeare, "To thine own self be true" really applies in this situation. Whenever you are not sure about something, you invite and open the door to experimentation on the part of the roommate. To avoid a bad experience, the more certain you are about what you will tolerate or not tolerate something is to have made a clear decision and your roommate will know exactly where you stand on the issue.

Uncertainty is your number one enemy as a landlord when dealing with a roommate situation. The more unclear you are, the more open the invitation the roommate has to experiment on you. It is important you have made a clear decision and are secure in your own self-knowledge ahead of time before you advertise looking for a roommate. If you do not know ahead of time what you will or will not tolerate or take from a stranger, this opens the door to "Pandora's Box", where anything that can happen –

eventually - probably will. If you are of this type of uncertain, unclear mindset, this is a danger to both yourself and a stranger coming to live inside your home. This uncertain, unclear thinking in "waiting to find out" from somebody else when they are inside your home living there with legal rights - is definitely not the time to discover you are not ready for a roommate. By the time that discovery about yourself takes place, you are too late!

This important "self-discovery" phase is the first step you should do before wasting money, time and energy placing advertisements looking for a roommate or even if it is a friend or someone you know. Often people tend to rush or overlook this critical phase, especially if the potential roommate is a friend or someone they know like a boy or a girlfriend. Always, always, always do this critical first step of "self-discovery" before you rent your room out in your living situation to anyone, friend and/ or boy or girlfriend included. Doing self-discovery work will save you a lot of headache, time and heartbreak from becoming roommates with the wrong person, friends included. Having a boy or a girlfriend move in with you right away without thinking about the all of the potential consequences of doing such a thing may hurt you if you do not take the time to know your own self first and what behaviors you will or will not tolerate inside your own home.

Or if you wait until you need the money so badly that you are willing to overlook this vital step of self-discovery and rush to get the first person who answers the ad and gives you money, this will hurt you in the long run. Waiting until a financial disaster hits you and then you look for a roommate out of financial desperation does put yourself and other people in your family in serious danger. I do not recommend – ever – waiting until your financial situation has gotten so desperate (you are about to be evicted or you fail to pay the mortgage for several months) before you decide to get a roommate. I never recommend anyone rushing into a hasty advertising campaign to fill your vacancy for some quick cash. Rushing behavior is irresponsible, reckless and endangers yourself and your loved ones, especially in a roommate situation.

This critical first step of "self-discovery" is so important of a concept to understand before you look for a roommate. Clearly defining your limits ahead of time of what you cannot stand and must have in your own personal living space is very important for you and your loved ones. These two steps in this chapter are meant to help you narrow down and narrowly define your own personal criteria of what you will and will not tolerate in a roommate. Remember, the more certain you are that you either like or cannot tolerate an item when doing these steps, the more empowered and readier you are to start looking for a roommate. The more uncertain, unclear, hesitant or unsure you are about what you will or will not tolerate in an item, the more you should consider not looking for a roommate as it is important you have a solid definition of what you will tolerate before inviting a stranger to come live in your home. Finding a roommate is not as simple as getting money from somebody. A roommate situation is truly not a workable living situation for everybody. It is my hope that by your self-discovery of what you will and will not tolerate in someone else, you see for yourself whether you are genuinely ready to take the next step in finding a roommate by doing these two steps in this chapter. These two steps are meant to help you in either case, make a final decision at this moment in time as to whether or not you are ready to look for a roommate. These steps will help the undecided "fence sitters" take a stand – one way or the other. And that is my goal in helping you to clarify for yourself, first of all if you are really ready to have a roommate. Within the next few pages, you will find two steps designed to get you thinking about behaviors that you will or will not tolerate from a roommate living in your house. There is no right or wrong answer to any of these questions, just the human variable of what you will or will not tolerate under your own room in your living situation.

Part 2 - The Second Step: How to Set Your Length of Rental Time, Security Deposit and Rent Fees Appropriately.

Now that you've done your honest self-examination in the last chapter of what you will tolerate and not tolerate from a roommate, the next step is to define how long you want your roommate to be on a lease agreement with you, the amount of the security deposit and the rent that is appropriate for your particular situation. If you did the two steps in this chapter, by now you should have a clearer picture of your own personal tastes and preferences for your own living situation. If you skipped doing those steps, I hope that you are starting this chapter with confident self-knowledge of clear boundaries.

If you are not sure or are uncertain about anything, I highly recommend that you go back and visit the last chapter, read what I say about uncertainty and the danger that unclear boundaries, uncertainty, lack of clarity or lack of decision does to a roommate situation. Hopefully by the time you read this chapter, you are very clear within yourself about what you will tolerate and not tolerate from a stranger who will be renting a room inside your living space from you and sharing it with you. Length of rental time, security deposit and rent fees are obviously different variables for everybody, depending on your personal living situation, and your local and state laws. Therefore, I will address issues in general that arise regarding these three topics in this chapter when looking for a roommate. How much rent should you ask? The best advice I can give you is for you do your homework and research the going rents in your local marketplace. Along with that research, find out how much the security deposits are in your area. You can also do this by checking out some websites like craigslist.com for your local area and read the ads for roommates. Once you have looked at ads in the newspapers and on the internet in your local area for roommates, you should have a ballpark idea of how much you can expect to get in rent for your particular situation. You want to charge more rent if you offer more private space or private use of things besides just a bedroom. If you have a private room with its own bathroom, rents are usually higher for a rental like that than in a situation where a bedroom has no private bathroom and you both have to share a bathroom. Also, if your private room has its own separate entrance, a patio and/ or a private yard, you should charge a little more rent than just for a private room and bath. The other situation that can happen is that you probably have seen ads that have another fee added on top of the rent in the format of "plus one-half, one-third or one-fourth utilities." This phantom "utilities" fee is a pet peeve of mine. I am sure it bothers potential roommates when reading a vague ad written like that because utilities change each month. This unknown factor adds unnecessary anxiety to an already anxious, nerve-racking process for both of you. In today's uncertain economic times, people want to know concrete answers. Vague fees that can vary from month-to-month turn off a lot of potential inquiries from an ad that advertises that "plus … of the utilities" wording. When you advertise your rental, I highly do not recommend putting a separate utilities fee in your ad at all. I do not care if fifteen other people are renting out your place, too. Most successful property managers keep things simple and straightforward. Potential renters know that also. So, this rule is not negotiable. I understand as a landlord myself that "it's not fair...." theory and people should pay for what they use. This is the answer to your shared utility problem: add all the utilities you offer to a roommate into the rent. One simple, flat rental fee is so much easier for both you and a roommate, especially if you both work and are busy. So, say for example, you have a room and a private bath for rent. The going market rate without a utility included (read the ads that do have the "include utilities" to adjust this figure) is, let's say $ 400 for a room on average. Then look at your ads that only have one flat fee. Figure the average amount that those people are paying. (Assume in those ads that utilities are included in the rents). Say that dollar amount comes out to $ 500. Next, you want to then take both figures and average them together to come up with one set amount that includes the utilities from both types of rentals. In this example, that average amount which would include the utilities would be $ 450. That is the average of both types of rentals. You should get as close as you can to the average amount to advertise for your rental, including the utilities. The reason for finding this average amount is that in those flat fee ads, usually those landlords are already including the utilities in their rental. To be sure, you can always call the landlord, pretend you are an interested renter and ask him or her if the fee in the ad includes the utilities. As a landlord, what utilities should I include in the rent? While you are not obligated to pay for someone else's phone, internet or cable bill, you should include in your utilities the electric, water, gas, sewer and any garbage fees. If you have a private yard that is included with the room and a landscaper maintains it, include a landscaping fee if you feel the roommate should either pay for maintaining the yard or offer the roommate to do the maintenance him or herself. You do not have to pay for internet access, satellite tv, cable or phone for your roommate. If you do happen to provide these extra "perks", do make sure you increase your rent amount to reflect that extra perk included in the rent. And a note of caution here: never offer as a perk - to pay for someone else's phone. This is just asking for trouble. While you are not obligated to provide little extras like perks, sometimes when a landlord does provide them, the room will rent faster because those little perks like internet access, cable or satellite tv attract people. So, do keep in mind the pluses and the negatives to renting your room out with or without these perks. Just make sure to increase the rent to help cover their half of the expense.

How long should I rent my room out to this roommate? What type of time length is the best in a situation like this? When you are getting a roommate, I highly suggest that you do a month-to-month length of rental time. However, how you decide to set the type and length of rental you will allow a roommate to stay on your property is your individual choice. My own experience shows that anything longer than a month-to-month basis may also give your roommate more legal recourse in a court of law, depending on your local laws and what state you live. I have found in my travels that most people usually do a month-to-month rental as these written contracts allow more leeway for sudden and unexpected life situations that happen beyond both your and your roommate's control. I do not recommend getting a longer lease from a roommate as life happens and it can be an uncomfortable position for both you and a stranger to live together for longer than a month-to-month basis. By doing a month-to-month type of rental, you also protect yourself in the event that things do not work out. You can get the roommate out of your place in a shorter amount of time than let's say a six month or a year lease. Although you may have heard of longer types of leases done in a roommate situation, I recommend staying away from anything longer than on a monthly basis. Also consider the fact that in case your roommate's family has an emergency situation that develops and he or she has to leave suddenly on a moment's notice without moving out of your place, you do not want the hassle of someone legally tying up your space which prevents you from being able to re-rent your place out to someone else. Also, in the event that someone decides to not pay the rent, a longer lease usually will give you more problems in handling the situation due to a longer time period involved which can be highly uncomfortable to both parties. It is best to avoid longer rental contracts for these reasons.

Turo

How TURO Works

TURO is a platform connecting people. There are two types of people on this platform: "Owners" and "Renters".

Owners are people who own the vehicle(s) and rent the vehicle(s) out.

Renters are those who do not have a vehicle but need one and rent it from Owners.

Both Owners and Renters alike must create an account and profile through TURO.

The Owners then make their vehicle(s) available to Renters. Then Renters can search all different types of vehicles available in the target market. This is all done through TURO's platform via the smart phone app or TURO.com. From there the Renter can search for a car that meets their needs and request to book a trip from the Owner.

Who May Utilize TURO

Anyone may utilize TURO as long as they create an account, which will require them to have a valid driver's license, active debit/credit account, and a decent driving record. The age limitation is 18 years and older, and some owners will limit their cars to be rented from renters 25+ years old, at their discretion.

Insurance and TURO

Insurance for the owner is 100% taken care of by TURO and their policy. TURO's policy goes up to 1 million dollars in value of coverage. This is more than enough for the average vehicle. If/when there is an accident caused by the renter, the renter simply reaches out to TURO support and notifies them of the incident. Then the renter will also reach out to the owner and notify them as well. If the renter fails to reach out to the owner TURO will absolutely reach out to the owner no matter what. From here TURO takes over and they initiate their process to deal with such circumstances. We will cover more of this process in the Renters Gone M.I.A., Missing Cars, and Accidents chapter in a little bit.

What Cars May be Listed?

Any car that does not exceed $75,000 in value and is a 2006 or newer with 100,000 or fewer miles qualifies. Both manual and automatic are included here as well, anywhere from 2-seater sports cars to 7 passenger vans. Apart from the contractual agreement you enter into when you create a TURO account is that the car you list must be in excellent operational status. There is a $100 fine if you list a car that has an issue that you knew about but did not disclose if the issue causes a problem for the renter. So, don't do this; be honest and transparent.

TURO and Their Cut

TURO will take 25% of the daily price after any discounts like weekly and monthly discounts. This is a far more than fair cut. They provide a one-million-dollar insurance policy for your car and live up to it, they provide amazing customer service and respond quickly, and let's not forget they provide a way for you to make largely passive income!

How You Get Paid

When you set up your account with TURO they will request you connect a checking account to your TURO account. They will then pay your earnings 3-5 days after the trip ends. It normally takes 2-3 business days for the payment to post to your account, though this will depend on your bank. If you have a trip lasting longer than one week, they will pay you out one week's portion 3-5 days after the end of the first week then another week's portion 3-5 days after the end of week two until the trip is complete. With seven cars we get paid some portion of funds about every 1-2 days.

Listing a Car

We started with listing one of our two cars on a part time basis. When we realized this platform was more than paying for our monthly car loan, we started to purchase additional cars to make a return. So, are you ready to list your car? Perfect! Let's make some money! First you will need to create an account. I will give you $25 towards your first rental by creating an account here. Once you create your account you may "List Your Car" and TURO will take you through a process of gathering and creating information about your car: its location, availability, photos, and description. Go ahead and do this now. We will then go over some things to tweak to make the system work best for you and to maximize your profits around your schedule. Don't worry about making the listing perfect. Over the next few sections we will go over every little detail to make it the best it can be. So, have fun and come back when you have created your profile to list your first car!

Setting Up the Calendar

For those who are looking to simply offset their monthly car payments, create a little cash on the side, and still need to fully rely on the listed vehicle as their primary transportation, setting up the calendar efficiently is critical. If you fail to do this you absolutely will get trips requested during a time you need your vehicle and you will have to cancel the trip possibly acquiring a cancellation fee from TURO. So, let's not do that. I will show you how to best optimize your calendar to fit your needs.

You will have to build the habit of daily updating your car's calendar in the smart phone application. You do this in the app by tapping the car in the bottom right corner<Calendar<Mark Calendar as Up-To-Date. If you need to add any "unavailability" to your cars calendar, like

if you have a doctor's appointment or are going out of town, then you simply tap the date on the Calendar<Add Unavailability. If you know your schedule for say a month out and want to update your calendar all at once so it is accurate and complete then you may do that as well. However, all renters will be able to see the last time you updated your calendar. So, if it was 3 weeks ago, even if the information is still relevant and correct, it could also send the message to your renter that you are not active.

Hours of Availability

Hours of availability are found on TURO.com (not in the app) under calendar. Here is where you may let TURO know your time frame you are ok with your guest's trips to start and stop. For instance, if you say your car is available 7AM-10PM a Guest will only be able to select to start their trip at or after 7AM on their desired day and may end their trip no later than 10PM on their desired day. Think of it like Hertz and the hours they are "open for business." This will also impact your ability to maintain a healthy "response time" in regards to getting back to renters who request to book a trip with you. If you choose to deliver the car, this will impact the times of day you are available to do this. Initially I did not know to account for response time. Then someone requested to book my car at 3AM for 6AM the same day, just 3 hours later. I obviously missed this request and my response rating went from 100% down to 98%.

I encourage you to simply put the hours of availability within your average daily wake up and sleep time. For instance, I normally wake up at 6AM daily and I go to sleep at 10PM. This guarantees I will be available to respond to a booking during the time I am awake.

Uber

Uber is a rideshare business that came from the yellow taxi idea but has some not so traditional methods of catching your ride. It wasn't always that way, as Uber was once just a California Dream and operating only in California. This is where their corporate office is still based out of. The application company in which regular people with no type of taxi or chauffeurs license can become a driver and have people in their local area contact them to pick them up in their personal cars.

As a rider, you can get a car of any type, from your average everyday Toyota to your van or SUV to even luxury vehicles like BMW's, pick you up within a matter of on average about 3-7 minutes, pick you up from your location and take you to a destination within the same city as well as outside the city and into another city or state.

How Uber Works for Drivers

Uber is a great way to make some extra spending money or even a full-time income for someone that wants to become self-employed operating their own business by their own standards. The process that Uber drivers use after they have sign up as a driver and approved by Uber is to simply download the Uber App to your smartphone. Whenever you're ready to work you simply turn your app on. There are no set hours to work a day it's as simple as turning the app on and off.

Once your app is on you will receive a ping which in Uber terminology is a request for a ride from a rider. You have 15 seconds to answer that ping (you are not required to answer pings). If you do not answer then the rider will have to request another ride and it will go to the next driver close to them unless you are the only driver then it will come back to you again. Again, you don't have to answer. But once you decide to answer a ping, the app will tell you how long it should take you to get to the rider and Google Maps or whatever you have set up for your navigation on your phone will pop up and give you directions to the rider.

Some drivers will call or text the rider to let them know that they are on the way, while other drivers will just arrive. Don't worry as Uber uses a temporary phone number to connect the rider and driver until the trip is finished.

Summary and Actions

Do you already drive with Uber or Lyft? Do you have spare chunks of time you want to monetize? Does making $60 in three hours sound appealing to you? Just like Colin, you can easily earn over $1000 a month by occasionally delivering goods when it's convenient for you. Sign me up (wait… I already am).

Honorable Mentions:

- Caviar
- Citizenshipper

- Deliveroo
- Eat24
- People Post
- Roadie
- Shyp
- Zipments

Platform Stacking: Delivery in the sharing economy is built for platform stacking. This is true more than any other sharing economy category. If you drive for a ride-sharing service like Uber or Lyft, it only makes sense that you also consider delivering goods during quiet ride-sharing periods. Likewise, if you are looking to make a few extra bucks while walking dogs on DogVacay, why not consider fulfilling walking deliveries on one of the many platforms above? Maybe the dogs can carry a bag or two.

You get the point; this is not rocket science. Seriously consider the delivery option to fill spare timeslots during your day.

CHAPTER 2

---≋---

GET AHEAD IN LIFE

Wealth creation starts with saving money. An individual's ability to save money can shape their lives and the lives of their families in many ways. Unfortunately for most people, the act of saving money is a challenge.

Modern society does not encourage or celebrate a savings culture. The U.S. savings rate has steadily declined for a number of years, before recently rebounding back over 6% in the wake of the recent economic crisis. Popular culture has focused more on earnings and lavish spending, instead of wealth creation. This has caused most Americans to engage in wealth destruction, instead of wealth creation. This is because wealth creation is a lifestyle, not a process. If you ask many teenagers and young adults what their interpretation of the word wealth is, they will probably point to someone who drives a luxurious car, a reality television star, or some highly paid athlete or artist.

Doesn't this sound more like lifestyles? There is never a discussion on regarding their savings habits. We never hear about a football player's investment strategy; unless they didn't invest wisely and lost everything. If a generation of individuals doesn't know what to strive for, how do we expect them to do anything but lose?

Re-learning Wealth Creation

No one wants to be in a situation where what they built up financially over a lifetime can be erased in mere months. They want to be financially healthy to the point where they can survive, and strive, in any market conditions. Unfortunately, most people don't know how to accomplish this. People typically understand that they earn money and then pay expenses. They usually don't give thought to the best way to spend money. There isn't much concern as to whether or not they are limiting their taxes, whether they are making smart purchases, whether or not they are investing enough, whether or not they are over-insured, or whether or not they are building wealth.

There are numerous benefits to creating a sound financial plan. However, there is no "one-plan-fits-all" to achieve this. There are many variables that have to be factored in, and an individual has to weigh them all. People with families will have a different set of priorities than someone without children. Young adults will have different goals than someone with less than five years until retirement. Situations aren't the only variables. An individual's current amount of debt, or their housing situation, or simply their lifestyle goals and habits will also impact any plan creation. Whichever road someone takes to build their financial future, it has to be attainable and reasonable.

Lifestyle and Wealth

As stated earlier, lifestyles have a profound impact on personal finances. The term lifestyles, in this case, can apply to a person's likes, dislikes, and habits; however, it will also apply to the set of circumstances that exist for an individual. This set of circumstances influences the daily decisions that an individual makes. Some of these items are non-negotiable. If you have children, it is hard to manage without buying diapers. If you have to commute to work, you are going to incur transportation costs. Owning a home has its own set of expenses accompanied with it. Personal habits will play a significant part in how you ultimately spend your money. Below are a number of profiles that most Americans fit into.

Young Adults (20's)

Young adults are just starting off and typically rent. They are single, and therefore, only have to be concerned with themselves financially. Their lifestyles are typically centered on finishing school or starting their careers. Cellular plans, eating out, and entertainment are the more common variable expenses that young adults incur. Saving for life's next phases, marriage, children, home ownership, and retirement seem less immediate, and are often overlooked.

Young Married Couples (under 30)

These couples are just starting out life together and are thinking heavily about buying a home and starting a family. If they are college grads, they may be carrying the baggage of student loans. They are transitioning from being young adults, and may struggle to give up some of their 'must-have's like extensive cell phone plans, designer clothes, or luxury cars. Sometimes, their income can support these items, but more often than not, this behavior is detrimental to future savings.

The Married Homeowners (aged 30-50)

A large portion of the US population is made up of married couples that own their own home. They have children and like to go on vacation every year. Their homes are filled with electronic gadgets and they have two cars in the garage. They are worried about saving for their retirement and their children's college costs. Many live in the suburbs and commute to work. Some opt to live on one income to save in child care expenses, while others require continuing with two incomes.

Divorced

Statistics show that almost half of all marriages in the US will end in divorce. Planning for this is difficult because no one ever thinks they will get divorced, or else they wouldn't get married. However, this life-changing event can be catastrophic to one's financial health. Typically, emotions cloud someone's ability to make sound financial decisions during this time. One person will be left managing a home that two people could barely afford. In addition, perhaps children are involved, and now these parents have to come to terms with raising a family while the parents are separated. To be sure, many people do this; it just becomes more difficult to manage your finances.

The Unmarried (over 30)

Sometimes you don't find the right person, or perhaps you have had no inkling to get married. Lifestyles will sometime continue to look like young adults; however, the earning potential for this group is much higher given how their career has progressed over time. As their incomes have grown, so have their toys. Perhaps they want to travel more, or live in an upscale area. They may have even purchased a home along the way. There are pitfalls out there though. Every so often, love finds a way to smack the unmarried across the face and they decide to settle down and start a family. Having a child in your 40's means guarantees college costs in your 60's. Your previous lack of preparation and savings means that you will be spending the rest of your adult life catching up.

Retired

Fixed incomes dominate this phase of one's life. If you haven't examined your spending habits before, attempting to live and plan with a fixed income brings these issues to the forefront. A lifetime of dependable savings habits will not only make this transition easier, but would have also allowed for wealth creation throughout your life. Wealth creation will diminish your reliance on a fixed income. Less reliance on a fixed income will improve your quality of life.

Single Parents

Becoming a single parent can happen at many different points in one's life. Whether a young mother or a divorced parent, the challenge is to stretch your income as far as you can to provide the best life for your family. Spending frivolously can have a dramatic impact on your family.

Not Just on Paper

Financial experts will often list a million different ways to save money, but they hardly ever take the time to show you how to put it into practice. Another issue, is that they don't often show who should be attempting these ideas or why. Everyone has different goals and dreams. Conversely, everyone has different problems. So, to tell someone that they should cut their grocery bills by 20% when they already have two growing children and the mother is pregnant doesn't make much sense.

Tips for Savings and Investments

As you continue with your fulltime employment, ensure that you should save minimum of 80 percent of your full-time job income to at least accumulate $50,000. This should only take your 1-2 years if done right depending on your income. Your side hustles should cover most or all of your expenses. Don't worry about investing for now and just keep grinding because it'll pay off.

CHAPTER 3

OBTAIN FINANCIAL
INDEPENDENCE

Most people list money as the single greatest source of stress in their lives. Yet, many have no desire to learn more about the underlying source of that stress and how to minimize it. Even more people are overwhelmed by contradictory advertisements and the non-stop barrage of sensationalist news stories. Everywhere you look there is someone telling you about hot stock tips or secrets on how to make money online. It's no surprise that the same people who are stressed out about money are also found muttering: "Investing? Saving? Ugh. Numbers are for nerds and old people. I can't be bothered."

Financial independence (FI), involves doing research, learning about yourself, and doing some (not too onerous) work to determine the relationship that you want to have with money. It requires investigating the sources of happiness in your life and setting priorities that allow you to maximize the happiness you'll receive from them. It means both understanding the psychological impact of modern consumerism culture and calculating how much money you need to stop working. And yes, there will be some numbers along the way, but don't worry. It'll be worth it.

Despite growing economic inequality, citizens of any western country in the 21st century are the wealthiest and most fortunate humans to ever have existed. Technology and real wage growth advances allow us to live lives that weren't even imagined one hundred years ago. Surely, if our great-grandparents knew the kind of lives we would live now, with a laundry machine in every home and 8-hour work-days, they never would have guessed that we would be so worried about money. So why do most of us feel like we'll never have enough?

Financial independence to me was defined as having enough capital and passive income that my financial needs were taken care of, regardless of the amount of labor that I do. Simply put, you have reached FI once you have a sum of money that is large enough to work for you (by bringing in income) so that you are no longer reliant on **your** work to make ends meet.

For some people, being FI may coincide with retirement, but that's not a requirement. Having your expenses covered means that money is no longer a source of stress in your life. But you don't have to achieve FI to obtain these psychological benefits. Even making progress towards your financial security, and eventually your full financial independence, can allow you to untangle the strong emotional and psychological association between money and happiness and brings you closer to self-actualization.

Here we turn back to our high school psych class and Abraham Maslow, an American psychologist, who says once you have saved at least saved 6-12 months of your expenses you can say you're financially independent which mean you don't have to live paycheck to paycheck.

How do you get to FI? Well, everyone's got their own ideas. We all know people who swear by real estate or proclaim that "the only way to make it big is to start your own business!" It can be a daunting thing to even think about. Investments can seem like mysterious black boxes and financial advisors appear to purposefully explain things in the most complicated way possible.

The truth is that FI is not an art. It's a science. There is empirical, peer-reviewed evidence available to answer almost every question you have about money, psychology, and the relationship between the two. Ignore the newspapers and the advisors getting rich off of your hard work. Let's stop guessing and get it right. Let's apply the scientific method to your money so we can properly answer both of these questions.

Investing is done by simply buying the type of investment you want to add to your portfolio. For stocks, some bonds, and other things requiring a broker you will need to hire one. This can be done physically by going to a financial office, or it can be done online. Typically, an online brokerage is less expensive but it also comes with a less personal touch. It is up to you to decide how involved you need your money to be managed. Note that the more that your portfolio is individually maintained the more you will be charged in fees. Often the fees can seriously cut into your profits, so consider buying investments through discount brokers or investing in assets that are not actively managed.

For other types of investments such as treasury bonds, you purchase assets directly through the organization you wish to invest in. Right on treasurydirect.gov you can create an account and purchase various types of investments without a broker. Overall the way that you purchase investments differs as per each type, but the best thing to do is sign up for an all-in-one type investment platform such as Vanguard. Through these services you can purchase stocks, bonds, mutual funds and more for a small fee and choose whether it is actively managed or not.

CHAPTER 4

——— ≈ ———

HOUSE HACKING

Real estate is another excellent way to invest your money. It differs significantly from the stock market, and there is also a variety of options. This next section will cover different types of real estate investment including the pros and cons of each, the risk level and the potential gains.

Once you saved at least $50,000 it's time to look for a multi-family to invest in. Depending on where you live, you might need more or less. Using the house hacking technique, get a duplex and you can live for free and rent the other unit out. Make sure the numbers make sense and cover your mortgage.

Now that you are living for free pretty much, you will be able to save more with your daily grind. At this point you need to get another source of income.

Owner- Occupant

This is a strategy that is a good idea for those starting out in real estate. It's great if you have the money to invest but want to minimize the time and effort you spend on maintenance and management. Here's what to do: buy a multifamily building with 2 or 3 units in it. You live in one of the units and the rent out the others. That way, if people need repairs you'll be right there. You won't need to travel across town to manage things and you'll be able to keep an eye on the place to make sure it doesn't get damaged. One risk with real estate is that tenants sometimes treat the place they live in badly. They cause extra wear and tear and sometimes damage.

Direct Ownership

Direct ownership is the first option that most people think of when it comes to real estate. This is where you are buying the property yourself and are responsible for the down-payment and the mortgage. There is a lot of upkeep required, especially as you get started with this asset. If you want to rent out your property, you'll need to manage it and there is work and money associated with that. Eventually, you'll want to build up your assets and hire a property manager. At first, however, you won't necessarily have the means to do that, so be prepared to put in time and effort for the upkeep of this kind of purchase.

Real Estate Limited Partnership.

This is much like a real estate investment group, but it's different in that it offers you an exit strategy. In this scenario, you are financing the construction of a property. Here is how this is set up: a property manager serves as a partner and outside investors finance this project in what is called "limited partners." After the building is constructed the partners may receive cash payments as a return on investment. The majority of the money made in this type of investment comes after the property is sold. The limited partners are paid out for having fronted the money pre-construction. Here are the downsides: the property might now sell for the amount expected, so you might not make as much money as you had initially hoped. Or, it may take a long time for that property to sell.

Real Estate Investment Group.

This is a way to own properties without having to be the landlord. Here is how: a company buys, or it builds apartment buildings. Then investors buy one or more units in the building through the company. The company manages the units for a fee and the investor makes money on it over time. This option is ideal if you don't want to be a landlord but want to capitalize on the growing real estate market. Another advantage to this kind of investment is that some groups pool money and establish a vacancy fund in case they are unable to rent a unit. That way they still get their mortgage paid on time. Not all groups use this strategy, so you may have to face that risk on your own. The downside of this investment is that you will typically pay a lot of money in fees. As well, you'll want to make sure that the real estate company managing the building is strong and highly qualified. You want to avoid poor management which can lead to a high turnover or other problems which will cause you to lose money.

CHAPTER 5

— ※ —

MULTIPLE SOURCES OF INCOME

In here, we will cover the various options available to you as a beginner investor, and also discuss more advanced investment opportunities. You'll get to know the pros and cons of each type of asset and discover what is right for you now.

To get started we are going to look at the three main classes of assets on the trading market. These are stocks, bonds and cash.

Stocks, Bonds, Cash and Mutual Funds

Stock refers to ownership in a company. There are two main stock categories. There is size and there is location. Each class has its own level of risk. In terms of size, stocks can be classified as large, mid and small.

When comparing and contrasting stocks, bonds, cash and mutual funds, stocks are the riskiest of the four. There are two ways to make a profit on the stock exchange. First: as the value of the company increases so does the value of their stock, if the value of the company decreases the value of their stock decreases. There are also fluctuations that can be outside of the company's direct control. A crash in the market, for example, will affect everything regardless of how stable the company is internally. In general, however, when you buy an asset your money will increase or decrease depending on the business's successes and failures. You can also make money on this investment through dividends, which are paid out when a company does well.

Bonds are the second type of investment we are going to look at. A bond is a loan. The company, or the government, borrows money from investors by selling a bond. It's a contract where they agree to pay back the money in a predetermined number of years with a predetermined interest rate. The US government borrows money from the people in the form of bonds. Here is how bonds work to make you money. When interest rates decrease, the bond's value increases. Conversely, when interest rates rise, the value of the bond decreases. One very important thing to know about bonds is that unlike stocks, the longer the term, the higher the risk. However, as a general rule bonds are lower risk than stocks.

Cash is the third type of investment. This is the money you put away in a 401K. This is the lowest risk investment of the three, but it doesn't mean there is no risk. The risk with cash has to do with inflation.

Mutual funds are a combination of stocks, bonds and cash that have been selected and put together by professional advisors for a specific amount of risk, and reward. They are lower risk than stocks and bonds.

Now that you're familiar with the different types of assets, you can start to evaluate which types work best for you. Ideally, you want to balance risk and reward in your portfolio. You do this through diversification, which means holding lots of different types of investments. When determining how you want to diversity it's important to remember that taking more risk will yield a higher return. You want to "buy low and sell high" as they say. Since the market fluctuates by nature there are highs and lows over time you want to buy stock when the price is low, and then sell it when it's high. The general trend is for the market to go up, but it's difficult to predict the peaks and valleys along the way.

Investing in Precious Metals

Precious metals are known to be rare metallic chemical elements and, throughout history, they have been used for different purposes. These elements are considered to be of high economic value and nowadays the most common metals in the monetary market are gold and silver. But when we refer to precious metals, then ruthenium, rhodium, palladium, osmium, iridium and platinum must also be recalled in this area.

Gold is the most popular metal which is used in the jewelry industry, but it is also known for its important role in medicine, electronics, dentistry, and food industry. In the present, this metal is seen more as a real investment, because the current money system is going through a period of stress and more and more people believe that investing in precious metals will be a safe method for the future.

If you decide to invest in gold, you should adopt the best strategy and try to find the most profitable way, based on your needs. You can resort to the physical gold method of investment, which includes coins, bars, and jewelry, or choose the gold exchange-traded funds and the gold stocks.

Silver also has a special place in both coinage and jewelry systems, and it is well appreciated for its high electrical conductivity. This metal has an important role in the manufacturing of musical instruments and dental fillings, or in the mechanical ventilation. Like gold, silver was used as a currency, but compared with gold, the price of silver is rather uncertain.

There are numerous ways in which you may invest in silver, and if you do not know what choice to make, then you should ask for an expert's opinion. If you prefer a traditional method of investment, you could choose silver bullion bars, but if you would like to search for a new form of trading, then invest in silver coins. Other methods could be those of exchange-traded funds, bank accounts, shares in mining companies and more.

Due to the present effects of the financial crisis, investing in precious metals could be the best choice. When most people think of investing in precious metals, they usually choose the bullion method of investment, but this strategy varies depending on each requirement.

Even if platinum and palladium are also used for different purposes, gold and silver remain the reliable factors of investment itself. For those who are already used to investing in these metals, they are a means to increasing their portfolio and a trusted source for the future.

However, even if the demand for precious metals keeps on rising, it doesn't necessarily mean there will be an immediate spike in price. It depends a lot on their constantly changing supply levels, resulting from active mining as well as the aggressive selling by large stake holders.

You have to do quite a bit of your own research before making your purchases. You also have to provide a storage space that is safe and secure if you elect to park your money on coins or bullion. Investing in precious metals requires maintaining a long-term perspective, meaning you have to be prepared to weather short term market volatility.

Options

The last type of investment we will cover in this section is Options. They are what is called "derivative" securities. This means that their value is dependent on and derived from the price of another thing. Buying an option gives you the right to have first dibs, so to speak, on the sale of an asset. An option is a contract. It gives you the right to buy an asset for a specific price by a specific date. The interesting thing with options is that you are not obligated to buy or sell the asset. There are two types of options: a call option, which is the right to buy, and a put option which is the right to sell. Options are different from Futures in that futures obligate you to buy and sell at some later date. Options give you the choice or the "option," which is where they get their name.

CHAPTER 6

FIND YOUR NICHE

For some people, finding their perfect place in the world is easy. Everyone seems to know at least a few people who have always known what they wanted to do with their lives and who managed to set organized goals from an early age. There are also those who happened to be in the right place at the right time and got "discovered," and are now living out their personal dreams. If you are reading this book, chances are you have seen how fulfilling it can be to find your niche, and you are ready to work towards giving yourself that gift.

Creating a successful business involves finding a niche in two important ways:

- First, by following your own passions and instincts so that your business lines up with your desires, values, and skills.

- Second, by filling a need in the market either by providing something that no one else is providing or by being the absolute best at what you do.

For now, focus only on the first part. Worrying about how to distinguish your business from the sea of competition will come later in the process.

What Will You Enjoy?

Starting a business is a little bit like raising a child. The early stages require almost round-the-clock care, so it is imperative that you choose something to which you are willing to devote that kind of time. Lots of types of businesses can be profitable, but you will burn out very quickly if you are not having any fun.

To start out, think of some activities you enjoy in your free time and write them down. Use the workbook at the end of this book for guidance. Remember to not limit yourself by judging whether or not a particular activity would make a good business venture. Simply list everything you love to do, whether or not you think it is relevant.

Next, list any past work experience you have had that has been enjoyable to you. If there was a job you had in the past that you did not completely enjoy, try and list the aspects of the job that you did like. The idea here is to pick out attributes of jobs that have made you happy in the past so that you can hopefully bring some of those ideas into your new business.

When you look at your lists together, do you see any common themes? Do you see any work experiences you have had that could combine with your leisure activities and hobbies to make an enjoyable and profitable business? Do you have any new ideas as you review your lists? Write down anything else that comes to mind. It is truly amazing how many ideas can come from simply taking inventory of things you already love and know how to do.

What Would be Fulfilling?

If you are going to start a business and devote a large amount of time and energy to it, it should be something that is not only enjoyable to you, but something that also would add great meaning to your life. For example, for one person, listening to music and occasionally playing the guitar is fun and entertaining. To someone else, the chance to listen to music, make critical observations, and share a passion for music with others via songwriting and performing is what gives that person's life meaning. It fills his or her soul with joy to even think about music. To that person, starting a business that is related to the music industry would have the potential to be deeply fulfilling.

If you have ever had a time in your life when you have felt fulfilled, think about that time. Was it during a past work experience? Was it on a vacation? Was it while you were alone? With family? Doing volunteer work? Try to remember as many details as you can about the experience. As you do this, think about the specific actions that made you feel fulfilled and write them down. For example, if you felt most fulfilled while building houses for Habitat for

Humanity, was it the carpentry that really spoke to you, or the service to others?

Identifying Your Values

As you think about the details of what is truly meaningful to you, you will be building a list of your core values. Values are those internal principles that motivate you and drive your actions. Look at the list you made and see if anything needs to be added. For example, if you value the ideas of teaching and mentoring, add them to the list even if you have never had any specific past experience in those areas. You want to end up with a list of everything that is truly important to you.

The list may be long, so it will be helpful to put it in some sort of order. By evaluating the list and at least prioritizing the top five that are the most important, it will seem less daunting. It would probably be difficult to think of a business that completely encompasses every single one of your core values, but there are probably countless business ventures that would fulfill your top five. If you are having trouble distinguishing between certain values, try giving each one a score from one to ten and see which ones score the highest.

Comparing the Lists

Now that you have a list of things you enjoy and a list of your core values, you probably are going to start seeing some patterns. This stage can be incredibly fun and enlightening because all sorts of creative ideas will start to come up. By combining things, you enjoy with things you find meaningful and fulfilling, you will start to have some fantastic ideas for businesses you can start. Write them all down. There are absolutely no bad ideas at this point!

There are a few more steps to go in identifying the business pursuit that is going to be the best for you, but you are already well on your way. Take some time to reflect the work you have done. Planning a business cannot be rushed, and it is beneficial to take a day or so in between steps to make sure you have not left out any ideas. If you find yourself itching to get to the next step, take it as a good sign. Enthusiasm is vital, but so is pacing yourself!

CONCLUSION

The world has just opened up to you as an investor and entrepreneur with all the information you've gained. We started with a lay of the land in terms of the difference between saving money and investing money. Due to inflation, and the depreciation of the dollar, saving is not the way to go long term. To get yourself in good financial standing, start off with accruing a 6-month emergency fund. This will give you a strong foundation to stand on as an investor.

The second way to build you financial castle is through investment. Once you have your foundational savings and a steady online business or a strong source of income, decide on the kind of investing you want to take on. There is the stock market, mutual funds and real estate to choose from. We went into great detail on each of these types of investments to help you determine which one suits your goals and your resources.

The tools of investing and money making are simple and clear: learn as much as you can about companies, about the stock market, and about entrepreneurship. Read as much as you can to gain the intellectual fortitude you need. Then get out there and gain real life experience.

For families with a modest income range, securing a large sum of money seems out of reach- but investing serves as a great equalizer that can help anyone amass a great wealth. Investing your money is one of the most worthwhile things you can do in your life, and everybody should be letting their money work for them by investing it.

Moreover, this book has recommended a method of investing that takes very little effort. Armed with the investing knowledge in this book, you can turn small amounts of money into fantastically large amounts with very little effort.